Essential New York: A Tourist Guide on the City

By Michael Persaud

This book is dedicated to all my American relatives as without them residing in New York, I could not have made several trips to that wonderful city.

TABLE OF CONTENTS:

INTRODUCTION

I have lived for over four decades just north of the American border in Toronto, Canada. This has given me an excellent opportunity to visit one of the greatest cities in the world, namely New York City. It's the city that never sleeps because it seems to be going 24/7 non-stop with activity happening all the time.

The lights of Broadway shine the brightest because stage actors really feel that they have made it if they've graced one of the stages of the Great White Way. There are many plays which have become iconic because they have been staged on Broadway such as *Hamilton, The Phantom of the Opera, Cats, All That Jazz, A Chorus Line, The Lion King*, and *Wicked*. Most visitors to New York clamor to get tickets to any play that is currently on when they are in town. Who can blame them? Only the best actors can be seen in such amazing productions.

New York is made of many districts and neighborhoods many of which have become familiar to the world through movies, TV shows, and popular songs. Shows like *Welcome Back Kotter* and *Sanford and Son* in the '70s; *Barney Miller* and *Fame* in the '80s; and *Seinfeld* and *Sex And The City* in the '90s paint a really good picture of what life in the city is like. Also the longest sketch comedy show which has been on since the 1970's *Saturday Night Live* was originated and is still broadcast from NYC. Songs like "No Sleep 'Till Brooklyn" by The Beastie Boys, "Empire State of Mind" by Jay Z and Alicia Keys, "New York State of Mind" by Billy Joel, "New York New York" by the Chairman of the Board Frank Sinatra himself, and "New York Minute" by Don Henley have cemented what a great metropolis this city is. One of the most potent musical genres which is still going strong today was birthed in the inner city. That rebellious music is called rap and was the creation of disaffected black youth who found a new way of expressing themselves. The first hit from this new form was "Rapper's Delight" by The Sugar Hill Gang in the '70s, which gave way to "The Message" by Grandmaster Flash and The Furious Five in the '80s, which further led to an explosion of this musical style in the '90s and into the 21st century. In the Batman comics and series of movies the city has been given another moniker which is Gotham. There was even a TV series based in New York christened with that name. Of course, we also know it as "The Big Apple" its most famous sobriquet. It's probably the most talked about city on the planet. The 45th president of the United States, Mr. Donald Trump, also resides in the city in his famous Trump Tower.

I, personally, have visited New York seven times during my lifetime. As child, as a teenager, in my twenties, and then in my thirties and forties. The more times I visit this city, the more I realize how much it has to offer, and also the moxie that inhabitants of New York have. They are filled with such character you can feel it just walking down the street.

The city is also a sporting town. They have two baseball teams in the New York Yankees and the New York Mets; two NFL football teams in the New York Giants and the New York Jets; two National Hockey League teams in the New York Islanders (who play out of Long Island) and the New York Rangers (who play out of Madison Square Garden in Manhattan); two

National Basketball Association teams in the New York Knicks (movie director Spike Lee's favorite team) and the Brooklyn Nets; and one Major League Soccer team in the New York FC. Now that's what you call a sporting town!

The city is comprised of many different boroughs and neighbourhoods some of which are Queens, Brooklyn, Ozone Park, Chelsea, Manhattan, SoHo, Greenwich Village, Staten Island, Tribeca, Flushing Meadows, Forest Hills, and The Bronx are just a few.

In this book I will attempt to point out the most essential things to see and do when visiting New York. There are tons, don't get me wrong, but these might be the essentials if you only have a short window in your time when visiting. So sit back and bask in all the great things which make New York such a fabulous city!

SOME HELPFUL HINTS

1. If you're approached by people you don't know try to avoid them. Most New Yorkers are nice but there are some unsavory characters you want to avoid. One night when my wife and I were out for a bite to eat we witnessed a guy in a grey hoodie cover his head breaking into a car. You can never be too safe. Be vigilant but not paranoid.

2. The subway is the cheapest way to get around but can be a little bit complicated. But you can learn it with a little study.

3. If a taxi driver tells you they will negotiate your fare, don't go with them. They might overcharge you. They might promise one thing but renege and go back on their word. Only go with reputable cabs like the famous yellow ones. The independent ones can sometimes try to fleece you but I'm not saying all of them are like that. There are tons of honest taxi drivers in NYC.

4. When arriving at one of their airports only use the yellow cabs which the airport authority figures tell you to. The other limousines may not fulfill their promise. As I've been told they are not to be operating out of the airport.

5. There also some good souvenirs which you can buy for very cheap on the street. Keep in mind there are not authentic but bootlegs.

6. If you have a good map and you know where you're going you can practically walk to most places especially if you're in Manhattan. My wife and I did that while we were there once. It was quite an adventure and we saw quite a bit. Once, though, when I was on my own sans map I got lost.

7. If you're in downtown Manhattan and have to go to the suburb you will have a hard time getting a taxi. After you hail a taxi and instruct them that you're headed out of the downtown core most will be unwilling to drive there because it is unlikely that they can pick up another fare coming back into the city. And of

course time is money for taxi drivers like everyone else.

8. If you're a tourist in the city be sure to visit Guest Services or the Tourist Desk in department stores if they have one. Most will provide a card for you to get a discount just because you're a tourist. They value your patronage and that will encourage you to shop even more, therefore, benefitting their bottom line. Everyone wins!

9. If you're a bibliophile or an aspiring screenwriter and love printed matter you can get bootlegged movie screenplays for a song on the street. That's the entrepreneurial spirits of native New Yorkers. They will sell almost anything. Same goes with souvenirs. If you don't want to spend good cash on the expensive stuff like t-shirts in stores, you can probably get them for cut-rate prices from street vendors.

10. Tapings for some of the iconic shows broadcast from New York City are generally free so you can try to get some tickets for when you will be in town. This applies to such shows

as *The Late Show with Stephen Colbert* and *Good Morning America with Robin Roberts*. Please see **www.nycgo.com** for more details. The same site can provide you with some details on free things you can do while you're in the city. For instance, the National Museum of the American Indian in Lower Manhattan and the American Folk Art Museum are always free of charge. That's a bargain in anyone's books!

11. Interesting fact: There are 4 million books in the New York Public Library's two-level underground storage area. The book train which takes about five minutes to bring books up to users is worth $2.6 million. The train travels about 290 meters of vertical and horizontal rails over the library's eleven levels. The maximum weight each of the train cars carry is 13.8kg.

AIRPORTS

The New York Metropolitan area has three airports to service people flying in and out of this great city. There are two which are located right in New York. Those are **LaGuardia Airport** (located in East Elmhurst, Queens) and **John F. Kennedy International Airport** (located in Jamaica, Queens, and built in 1948), the latter named after the 35th president of the U.S., and the former was named for New York's mayor at the time it was built in 1953, Fiorello La Guardia . (LaGuardia is not the most cleanest airports you will ever travel through). All you would need is a taxi or an airport limousine to get to your hotel or accommodations if you flew into one of these airports. Be careful that your driver knows beforehand where your accommodation is before you leave the airport. For instance, there are two W Hotels which are in different directions in the city. As a traveling note: don't share a limousine or cab with other travellers you don't know. Since New York is a large city you might both be going in different directions which your driver may not wish to accommodate as he takes off from the airport. So one set of passengers may be left stranded and have to hail another taxi. The third airport is actually located in Newark, New Jersey and is called **Newark Liberty International Airport**. If your plane is flying into Newark Airport, be forewarned you will need ground transportation from the airport to get to New York City which will be rather costly. Likely over $100.

MUSEUMS

With the likes of Andy Warhol and Basquiat who were immersed in the New York art scene it's not hard to see that if artists hope to make a name for themselves they must get involved in the bohemian life that is prevalent throughout the city. New York probably has the most galleries than any other city in the world including cities which are found in Europe. The thriving art scene means you can see the latest and greatest artists today who are making a name for themselves. You can find avant-garde artists, those delving into abstracts, or who choose to ply their trade in realism, sculptures or photography. The New York art scene is thriving and since it is so eclectic it dwarfs art scenes around the world. Here are some of the more larger and more well-known art galleries which will enable you to sample some visual art in the city.

Museum of Modern Art (MoMA) – 11 West 53 Street – www.moma.org

It's at a new location which it moved to a few years ago. The building it's housed in is completely white and stands out. On the highest floor is where you would see the latest exhibit. When I was there it was some of the Old Masters from Europe. On the lower floors you can see some Picassos, Van Goghs, Monets, and other great painters from the days of yore. There is also a floor for photography for those who love to take in still life. It's a large museum so take your time when perusing. Keep in mind you can take pictures on some floors but not all, please inquire when you're there. It has a second location in Queens known as **MoMA PS1** at 22-25 Jackson Avenue.

The Metropolitan Museum of Art (The Met) – 1000 Fifth Avenue – www.metmuseum.org

Probably the largest museum in the city, it's located in Manhattan near the famous Central Park. It has a great many works of Old Masters. Open seven days a week but only closed Thanksgiving Day, Christmas Day and New Year's Day plus the first Monday in May. Commonly referred to as "The Met" its collection is very wide and extensive. Has over 2 million square feet of art spanning over 5,000 years so it's quite extensive. Its art explores a lot of cultures and time periods. You can purchase your tickets online to beat the lineups. It has eight places where you can dine while there: The Cafeteria, Petrie Court Café, The American Wing Café, Roof Garden Bar, Great Hall Balcony Bar, The Balcony Lounge, Members Dining Room, and Members Rooftop Bar (only open during good weather). It has three locations: The Met Fifth Avenue, The Met Breuer (945 Madison Avenue), and The Met Cloisters (99 Margaret Corbin Drive).

Solomon R. Guggenheim Museum (The Guggenheim) -- 1071 Fifth Avenue – www.guggenheim.org

This museum is sometimes referred to as "The Guggenheim" and displays mostly Impressionist, Post-Impressionist, early Modern and contemporary art. The museum was designed by renowned architect Frank Lloyd Wright and is mostly shaped like a cylinder. It has been amassing it's collection over eight decades and is located in the Upper East Side of Manhattan. It was founded in 1937 but built in 1959 and is a sister museum of the one of the same name in Bilbao, Spain.

The Whitney Museum of American Art --- 99 Gansevoort Street --- www.whitney.org

Initially founded by American sculpture Gertrude Vanderbilt Whitney in 1930 and opened officially in 1931. It has had many iterations since its early days but the last edition of the museum opened on May 1, 2015 where it now sits. The main premise behind the museum is to showcase American art. Artists in the United States were having a difficult time finding a forum for their work that's the reasoning behind Ms. Whitney's founding this wonderful museum. It currently has a permanent collection of 21,000 works which were the creation of 3,000 artists during the 20th and 21st centuries. The main thrust of the museum is 600 works which were created by the hands of Gertrude Vanderbilt Whitney herself. She passed on in 1942. Designed by architect Renzo Piano the museum's building is in the city's meatpacking district.

Museum of the City of New York -- 1220 Fifth Ave at 103rd St. – www.mcny.org

This museum is open seven days a week. Founded in 1923 as a private, not-for-profit institution, this museum celebrates all that is New York from the past, present, and what is to be the future. The museums main objective is to educate people about what New York is all about, the changing face of the city, where it came from concerning its past, how immensely diverse it is, and how it continually evolves. It hopes to bring this message not only to New Yorkers but tourists visiting the city through programs, its collections, exhibitions, and publications.

Cooper Hewitt, Smithsonian Design Museum – 2 East 91st Street – www.cooperhewitt.org

The Cooper Hewitt's main mission is devoted to design from the past as well as the present day. Its objective is to instill inspiration, give a forum for design, and hopefully inspire others to pursue design whether it be professional or as a hobby. It has many programs, exhibits, and continues to publish literature on the nature and the progression of design. It was founded in 1887 by the granddaughters of industrialist Peter Cooper namely Amy, Eleanor, and Sarah Hewitt. It has been a brand of the illustrious Smithsonian since 1967 and is currently in the Andrew Carnegie Mansion on Fifth Avenue. The collection has a total of 210,000 design objects and has a very extensive library as well. It offers educational programs and very interesting exhibits on anything involving design. It hopes to perpetuate the beauty and learning of the intricacies of design in the United States.

Museum of Sex -- 233 Fifth Avenue – www.museumofsex.com

Now that we have your attention with the name, let's explore what this museum is all about. Don't be shy, it's for everyone because without the act of lovemaking involving sex none of us would be here. The main thrust of the museum is to provide the history, evolution, and cultural significance of sex. The museum hopes to enlighten visitors with what sex is all about and hopes to educate and dispel myths around the most sacred act. It hopes this leads to further discussion about what sex really means to us as humans. The museum continues its mission through interesting exhibits, programs, and publications it puts out. Prudes as well as the more liberal minded are all welcome.

The Skyscraper Museum -- 39 Battery Place – www.skyscaper.org

New York out of any great metropolis in the world is filled with some of the greatest skyscrapers in the world. So it would be fitting that it would have a museum which celebrates such great edifices. The museum's main mission is to celebrate the architectural heritage of the city and the history behind many of the city's tall buildings. The main facets it delves into are the design, real estate, technology, and construction of some of these great buildings. It promotes this through its exhibits, programs, and publications. It hopes that the curious public would also like to learn the various facets of what constitutes and comes into play when a tall structure is being built from inception to completion.

Madame Tassauds New York -- 234 W. 42nd Street – www.madamtussauds.com/newyork

We would all like to be immortalized in wax someday that is if we become a cult of personality. The museum has innumerable wax figures which promote iconic people who permeate our cultural landscape and bring them to life in wax. The figures seem true to life. We're sure you would love to take a selfie or observe the intricacies in what goes into making some of these very detailed wax figures. You might see such figures as The Hulk, the beautiful Rihanna, the late Whitney Houston, E.T. The Extra Terrestrial, Iron Man, eminent director Steven Spielberg, and many more!

Brooklyn Museum -- 200 Eastern Parkway – www.brooklynmuseum.org

This museum is located but where else? Brooklyn! This museum attempts to enable you to experience the most dynamic and constantly changing urban centres of the world right here in Brooklyn. This museum is so eclectic it invites you into varied civilizations which include "…ancient Egyptian masterpieces, African art, European painting, decorative arts, period rooms, and contemporary art." It gives you a fresh perspective and lets you into the diverse nature of our planet and in so doing better shed some light on cultures which you might not normally come across in everyday life. One of its aims is to foster more learning through its exhibits and programs.

Brooklyn's Children Museum -- 145 Brooklyn Avenue – www.brooklynkids.org

Yes, another fabulous museum in Brooklyn, but this time dedicated to those of a more tender age. Its three floors of interactive exhibits encourage kids from 6 months old to 10 years of age to become more engaged with what they are seeing. It's actually the world's first museum dedicated to children. It was founded in 1899 and since its inception has led to the creation of over 300 children's museum's spanning the globe. The museum hopes to inspire kids, spark their imagination, get them involved in the fun of learning and hopefully to make them become lifelong learners. Society as whole would benefit.

New Museum – 235 Bowery – www.newmuseum.org

The New Museum attempts to bring to the fore the works of living artists. The New Museum was designed by Tokyo-based architects Kazuyo Sejima and Ryue Nishizawa, and is a seven-story white building which resembles something akin to off kilter building blocks. It's unique in its design but awe-inspiring to look at. Has great exhibits on contemporary art and offers an internship program and welcomes volunteers to give tours of exhibits.

New York Hall of Science -- 47-01 111th St., Corona, NY – wwwnysci.org

This hands-on museum is perfect for the curious and those who want to be immersed in learning more about science. With over 450 exhibits, demonstrations, workshops and activities to partake of they will help you learn more about STEM (science, technology, engineering, and math). Perfect for teachers and young minds who would like to expand their sphere of learning and broaden their mental scope about STEM.

Founded in the 1964-65 World's Fair it purports to help you learn more about these interesting fields which are paramount to also learning about our world.

Museum at Eldridge Street -- 12 Eldridge Street between Canal and Division Streets – www.eldridgestreet.org

The main objective of the museum is to continue to "restore and sustain the National Historic Landmark 1887 Eldridge Street Synagogue." It also hopes to foster the Jewish American traditions and culture in the diaspora, its rich history and continued thriving culture, city living along with new immigrants, and the various languages of preservation and architecture with this tradition. It offers walking tours and programs for those interested in learning more about the Jewish experience in America. Additionally, it offers concerts, interesting lectures, and wonderful festivals to better acquaint someone with this way of life.

The Paley Centre for Media -- 25 West 52 Street -- www.paleycenter.org

There is a sister location of this centre in Beverly Hills, California. Media is an integral part of our lives. We are surrounded by it every day. It promotes all that is important in our world. Media is one of the most enduring things that allow our culture and the world at large to survive and thrive as it does. The Paley Centre for Media promotes the learning of culture and social relevance in our lives, when it comes to television and radio, and all the other platforms which have been emerging with the growth and expansion of technology. Come open your eyes and ears and learn how and why this affects us as humans since we are thinking and discerning beings.

The Studio Museum in Harlem -- 144 West 125th Street -- www.studiomuseum.org

African-American culture is a very important part of American culture when you consider the contributions that African-Americans have made to the country as a whole. They add to the richness that is America. This museum connects the work of African-Americans on a local, national, and international level. Its main aim it to promote the growth and evolution of black culture. It hopes to do this through dialogue about art and society concerning the great works of those of African descent. It was founded in 1968 by a cabal of artists and philanthropists who wanted to display artwork but also be supportive of the creators of the work and also educating the public.

New York Transit Museum -- 99 Schermerhorn St, Brooklyn -- www.nytransitmuseum.org

New York City has one of the most famous transit networks in the world. In fact, it's one of its largest like the ones in Paris, France and London, England. It's very complex and will take some studying on how to use it efficiently. This museum celebrates all the New York Transit Authority represents and how it gets it millions of travellers around daily. The transit system never closes and runs 24 hours a day year round. This museum founded in 1976 brings to life the transit system from its early days to the present day. The museum covers all the engineering that went into making the system like a well-oiled working labyrinth and the technology and design that keeps it running to this day.

Queens Museum -- New York City Building, Flushing Meadows Corona Park -- www.queensmuseum.org

The formation of the museum is dedicated to the promotion of visual arts in the New York Metropolitan area but more specifically to the residents of Queens. The museum focuses on it rich cultural heritage and continual diversity from the international community and offers the love of the visual arts though programs and exhibits. It additionally likes to focus on the educational aspect and also collecting and exhibiting art including the areas of architecture and design.

Jewish Children's Museum -- 792 Eastern Pkwy, Brooklyn -- www.jcm.museum

Children are the lifeblood of our lives. It's important for us to educate and keep their minds inspired as they grow and even while they are still forming their consciousness. Museums like this celebrate that very fact: children are very, very important citizens of this world. This museum promotes the Jewish culture through education, exhibits and programs. It's a hands-on museum and is open to children and their families of all faiths. It's nice to learn about cultures outside of our own and this museum definitely provides that objective by letting young ones learn about what makes the Jewish culture so rich and immensely interesting.

Museum of Jewish Heritage -- 36 Battery Pl -- www.mjhnyc.org

The American cultural scene is rooted in a Judeo-Christian tradition. Jews have played a great part in the building of America through sectors such as business, religion, media, entertainment, literature, and the arts.

Just like other cultures which can be found in the American landscape, Jews are integral to what constitutes America. "The mission of the Museum is to educate people of all ages and backgrounds about the broad tapestry of Jewish life in the 20th and 21st centuries—before, during, and after the Holocaust." The museum offers new exhibits and special exhibits to promote the main aim of what it means to be Jewish. It also offers discussions, lectures, plays, and films to further enhance the general scope of how it promotes the Jewish contribution from a cultural standpoint and also through ideas that is disseminated through learning.

New-York Historical Society -- 170 Central Park West at Richard Gilder Way (77th Street) -- www.nyhistory.org

This museum was founded to promote and enlighten through programs and exhibits historical aspects which have come to shape our world. Its main objective is to bring forth the richness of New York City, New York State, and America and display its significance when it comes to politics, cultural and societal changes that have come to make the city, the state, and the nation what it is today. It tries to shape this through discussions about what has made America probably the most cultural influence in the world today. It offers exhibits and has a great collection as well. Its library alone has over 2 million manuscripts, 500,000 photographs, and 400,000 prints just to give you a good impression of the vastness of what it has to offer.

9/11 Memorial & Museum -- 180 Greenwich Street - - www.911memorial.org

September 11, 2001 was one of the greatest tragedies to every befall America and humankind. The searing memory of what occurred that day will forever be imprinted on the soul of humanity. Most people remember where they were when those events of that awful day unfolded. This museum is to remember the victims of two tragedies which occurred on February 26, 1993 and September 11, 2001. It is to remember those who helped, those who survived the horrific acts, and the friends who helped during one of the worst terrorist acts the world has ever seen. As the museum's website reads: "May the lives remembered, the deeds recognized, and the spirit reawakened be eternal beacons, which reaffirm respect for life, strengthen our resolve to preserve freedom, and inspire an end to hatred, ignorance and intolerance."

Van Cortlandt House Museum -- 6036 Broadway, Van Cortlandt Park, Bronx – www.vchm.org

The Van Cortlandt House Museum has been opened since 1896 and is a historic house. The interior of the house is meticulously maintained and as well as the collection it boasts. It offers educational opportunities for visitors as well as students from schools. The museum is open 6 days per week year round. It is held under the auspices of the The National Society of Colonial Dames in the State of New York. Please make note: the museum is occasionally closed to the public due to inclement weather, if it is being used for a film shoot, fallen tree branches, restoration projections or also problems due to the general maintenance of the home. Please call ahead or check their website.

American Museum of Natural History -- Central Park West at 79th Street – www.amnh.org

This museum is only closed two days out of the year: Thanksgiving Day and Christmas. Otherwise it's yours to enjoy any other time of the year seven days a week. They also offer self-guided tours to anyone visiting. Founded in 1869 the mandate of the museum is to continue the education of the modern world when it comes to its natural history, cultures, and the vast universe around us. Some of its permanent exhibits include those on fossils, biodiversity, reptiles and amphibians, dinosaurs, mammals and earth and space. So as is evident it covers a wide range. There are always special exhibits and new ones upcoming. There is also a Discover Room for those ages 5 to 12 which encourages the touch factor since it is hands-on.

The Cloisters -- 99 Margaret Corbin Dr, New York -- http://www.metmuseum.org/visit/met-cloisters

Specializing in European medieval architecture, sculpture and decorate arts The Cloisters is located in

Upper Manhattan and is affiliated with The Metropolitan Museum of Art. Its main focus is Romanesque and Gothic periods in history. It generally has four areas with it concentrates: the Cuxa, Bonnefont, Trie and Saint-Guilhem cloisters of which whose main source was French abbeys and monasteries. It tends to put forth the monastic life with respect to architecture, the museum itself is surrounded by wonderful medieval gardens. The Cloisters due to its remarkable beauty and history has been used in a number of films.

The Frick Collection -- 1 East 70th Street – www.frick.org

This beautiful art museum is home to the Frick Collection of former Pittsburgh industrialist Henry Clay Frick. It is located in Upper East Manhattan on Fifth Avenue. It features paintings of the Old European Masters plus includes some fine sculptures and decorative art objects, or if you will *objets d'art.* Some of the greats whose work you are likely to see at the museum include Bellini, Rembrandt, Vermeer,

Gainsborough, Goya, and Whistler. The museum initially opened its doors to the public in 1935. Frick's daughter has also established a great library for research. It is located adjacent to the museum and opened in 1920 by Helen Clay Frick. It was blessed with the name the Frick Art Reference Library and is considered one of the best in the world. The museum also has an educational outreach with its lectures and symposiums.

Intrepid Sea, Air & Space Museum -- Pier 86, W 46th St & 12th Ave -- www.intrepidmuseum.org

This unique museum differs from the rest because its main focus is on "...the legendary aircraft carrier Intrepid, the space shuttle Enterprise, the world's fastest jets and a guided missile submarine." Initially founded in 1982 its objective is to foster and continue the education and learning about American innovation in the areas of sea navigation, conquering the skies and the heavens above. The museum has over a million visitors each year and covers over 18,000 sq. ft. near the Hudson River.

ATTRACTIONS AND TOURS

Citypass – www.citypass.com/new-york-comparison

One of the best ways to see New York City. You can save up to 25% or 41% depending on which version of the pass you elect to go with. There are two versions on the Citypass website which permits you to see multiple attractions – either 6 attractions or 3 attractions – and save a lot of money while doing so. This is an excellent way to see The Big Apple and you will not have to keep fumbling for credit cards, debit cards, or money if you already have the pass in your possession. Great value!

GrayLine Sightseeing New York -- www.newyorksightseeing.com

This wonderful sightseeing company offers bus tours, helicopter tours, and boat tours. Great combination of choices for those wishing to get the full experience of visiting NYC. They also offer some great day trips if you're interested. This company has attractions and other fine packages to choose from on their website. Excellent selections of things to see and do!

HOUSES OF WORSHIP

Every city in this world that is a cultural mecca like New York has its houses of worship which not only hope to attract the faithful but the curious as well. These buildings are architectural wonders which have a certain resonance to them whether you're of the same faith, as those who come for services, or if you are of the mind that something special and unique resides within their walls. They were erected during the early years of the building of the city and still stand the test of time about their importance to the city that is the biggest "melting pot" in the world. Native New Yorkers come from all corners of the globe and regardless of the melanin, or lack thereof on their skins, many chose to visit these important houses where The Word is being preached. Regardless of whether or not you are from the same flock, as the adherents of these buildings, they still welcome your presence, and hope you have a good time while visiting their buildings. These buildings are so beautiful they will take your breath away.

Cathedral of Saint John The Divine -- 1047 Amsterdam Ave -- www.stjohndivine.org

One of the most gorgeous and captivating architecture structures you will find in all of New York City and not technically a museum, per se. Still functioning as a church it serves the diverse city of New York regardless of ethnicity. There are over 30 services per week which are attended by those of varying faiths. The church also serves over 25,000 meals per annum. It has many concerts, educational and outreach programs. It's one of the most divine structures that you will ever set foot in and one of the largest in all of New York City. The architecture itself will leave you speechless.

St. Patrick's Cathedral -- 5th Ave -- https://saintpatrickscathedral.org/

This too is not a museum but one of great houses of worship in New York and a breathtaking edifice. St. Patrick's Cathedral receives over 5 million visitors per year regardless of religious affiliations and the Archbishop claims that one million candles are burned during services every year. It has some gorgeous stain glass windows depicting scenes from The Bible. Both the interior and the exterior of the building are sights to behold due to the meticulous nature of its intricate architecture.

ZOOS

**The Bronx Zoo -- 2300 Southern Blvd, Bronx --
https://bronxzoo.com/**

Go wild! Bring the whole family because this is a place
where you will see some of the most gorgeous animals
with whom we share the planet. It's fun for everyone!
There is a Butterfly Garden, Aquatic Birdhouse and Sea
Bird Aviary, Baboon Reserve, African plains pavilion
where you can see lions, the Sea Lion Pool, the Congo
Gorilla Forest, the World of Reptiles, just to name a
few. There is also a Children's Zoo Area featuring
goats, alpacas, anteaters, and prairie dogs. There are
certain activities during the day which can be observed
by the public like the feeding of sea lions or penguins.
The Bronx Zoo also has a 4D Theatre for more
enjoyment. Especially good if you have young kids. It's
open year round so you always have a chance of seeing
all these majestic animals.

Central Park Zoo -- 64th St and 5th Ave -- https://centralparkzoo.com/

Here's another place where you can see some really gorgeous animals. If you are not within the vicinity of The Bronx Zoo when visiting, this is another great option. It's not as large as the Bronx Zoo but still it's worth the visit. They have only a few pavilions where you can observe animals going about their days: Allison Maher Stern Snow Leopard, Central Garden & Sea Lion Pool, Grizzly Bear and Treena's Overlook, Polar Circle where can see some diving penguins and some wonderful puffins, Temperate Territory, Tisch Children's Zoo (perfect for the little ones!) where you can see Nubian Goats or Pot-Bellied Pigs, and the Tropic Zone: The Rainforest. So as you can see it's quite eclectic and you will not be bored in the least. There are some feeding times which can be observed by visitors to the zoo.

IMPORTANT BUILDINGS

New York City has one of the most impressive and world-renowned skylines that is very impressive in its grandiosity. It has a great many buildings which dot its landscape and which made it appear as famous like Hong Kong's, Toronto's, London, England, Dubai's, and Paris, France. There are so many buildings it's a feast for the eyes and mind. Here are some which you should not miss on your sojourn to this great city, The Jewel in the Crown, of the United States.

The Empire State Building -- 350 5th Ave – http://www.esbnyc.com/

One of the most famous buildings the world has known. It at one time was the tallest edifice in the entire world. It has been surpassed by many in recent years but still has an enduring allure about it. Construction on it started on March 17, 1930 during the height of The Great Depression. It has also been featured in the movie King Kong where the mammoth beast hangs off of it with Fay Wray in one hand as he takes swipes at airplanes trying to save the damsel in distress. It's one of the first Art Deco buildings that made that gave the architecture movement its prominence. The Empire State Building has two observation decks, one indoors and one outdoors. Its Art Deco lobby murals have recently been restored. It has stores, restaurants, and a visitor's centre for patrons. A visit to New York is not complete without a visit to the Empire State Building.

Yankee Stadium -- 1 East 161st Street -- http://newyork.yankees.mlb.com/nyy/ballpark/

One of the most storied sports venues in all of professional sports and home to the legendary New York Yankees and also the New York FC of Major League Soccer. It is located in the Bronx. This current rendition of the stadium replaced the original (which had the same name) in 2009. It cost $2.9 billion to be constructed which makes it the most expensive stadium that was ever built to date. It also hosts college football games and music concerts.

Chrysler Building -- 405 Lexington Ave

Another one of the great Art Deco edifices that make the New York City skyline so fantastic. Its beauty is unmistakeable. At 1,046 feet it was once the world's tallest building until about 11 months later it was superseded by the Empire State Building in 1931. After the unfortunate destruction to the World Trade Centre in 2001 the Chrysler Building regained the second spot of being the tallest in height, until 2007 when it was surpassed by the Bank of America, which reached the awesome high of 1,200, then it was relegated to third spot on the city's skyline. Currently, it now stands in fifth spot with respect to height after the completion of One World Trade Centre and 432 Park Avenue in the year 2015. It was the headquarters for the Chrysler Corporation from the 1930s to the 1950s, however, the car company did not pay a cent for its construction. Walter P. Chrysler actually paid for it out of his own pocket, therefore, his children could inherit it upon his passing. Unfortunately, its old observation deck is no longer in use by the general public but they are permitted to have a tour of its lobby. These lobby tours can only be had from Monday to Friday from 8am to

6pm. The Art Deco murals, the beautiful clock, and elevators are great examples of this architectural movement.

One World Trade Center -- 285 Fulton St. -- https://oneworldobservatory.com/tickets

This remarkable building replaces the World Trade Center which was destroyed during the horrific terrorist attacks etched in history on September 11, 2001. Construction on it commenced in 2006 and it is located in Lower Manhattan. It currently sits at being the tallest building in the Western Hemisphere and holds the esteemed title of being the sixth tallest in the world. Its perimeter consists of four streets "…West Street to the west, Vesey Street to the north, Fulton Street to the south, and Washington Street to the east." Opening on November 4, 2014, its height is currently 1,776 feet which is symbolic of the year the United States obtained its independence. Some colloquially refer to it with the moniker "Freedom Tower." It consists of 104 floors but in reality it is only 94 actual stories in height. It has an impressive 73 elevators and cost $3.9 billion to construct. It does have an observatory opened to the public but there is a charge. Please see the website link in order to purchase tickets for your visit. There are various types of admission tickets so be cognizant when buying yours.

Rockefeller Center -- 45 Rockefeller Plaza -- www.rockefellercenter.com

Located in Mid-town Manhattan it is one of the most gorgeous buildings you will find. During the Holiday Season it has one of the most famous and tallest Christmas trees you will ever find. It also has a wonderful skating rink in the front of the building which people are welcomed to use. It consists of 19 high rise commercial buildings and came into being after it was commissioned by the very wealthy Rockefeller family. Built in the famous Art Deco design of the period construction on it commenced in 1930 during the height of The Great Depression and was completed 9 years later. The construction of the buildings involved an astounding 40,000 workers. Ownership has changed hands several times, the last was in the year 2000 when it was sold for a jaw-dropping $1.85 billion. The Rockefeller family no longer has a stake in it. NBC studios are currently housed in one of its buildings at 30 Rockefeller Plaza. If you would like a tour please visit its website above.

State of Liberty – located at Liberty Island in New York Harbor --
http://www.statueoflibertytickets.com/

Reaching just over 305 feet this amazing statue was a gift to America from France and was sculpted by the Gustav Eiffel. It was formally dedicated October 28, 1886. The statue itself depicts a female Roman goddess Libertas. The torch she holds is inscribed with the date of American's Year of Independence July 4, 1776. At her feet lies a broken chain. Her name in Libertas means "freedom" in Latin. The Statue of Liberty was a welcomed sight for immigrants fleeing persecution or various social ills in Europe hoping for a better life for them and their children. It has been restored three times due to natural decay and withering of the statue. Architecturally it is considered neoclassical in design.

For tickets to this awesome structure please visit its website above.

Carnegie Hall -- 881 -- 7th Ave -- https://www.carnegiehall.org/

One of the most popular performing arts venues in the world, this building has seen some greats in its time. It consists of three stages for the promotion and continuation of music and the cultivation of the love of music. It is accessible for those with physical, auditory, or visual challenges. Please visit its website for more information. Its Rose Museum onsite allows visitors to see the history of Carnegie Hall through photos, videos, and other ephemera that celebrate its rich heritage. The Hall is closed July 1st to October 1st every year.

Radio City Music Hall -- 1260 -- 6th Ave – www.radiocity.com

Declared a city landmark in 1978 it was once considered *the* place to be in New York. Part of the famous Rockefeller Centre it is home to the world famous New York City Rockettes which are a Christmas holiday favourite in *The Radio City Christmas Spectacular* if you're ever in the city during that special part of the year. It has been branded with the sobriquet "Showplace of the Nation" and it's an apt moniker considering it has seen many luminaries grace its stage. Its seating capacity is just over 6,000 patrons and it is also built in the very well-known Art Deco architecture design of the period. It offers walking tours for a behind the scenes look at what makes the venue so great. Please check their website for prices and times.

Madison Square Garden -- 4 Pennsylvania Plaza – www.thegarden.com

Home to the New York Rangers of the National Hockey League (NHL) and the New York Knicks of the National Basketball Association (NBA), it also has hosted some of the greats in the entertainment world. It is the fourth iteration of a venue graced with a similar name and sits atop Pennsylvania station in Mid-town Manhattan. It also has hosted circus acts, professional boxing, some amazing musical acts, and spectacular ice shows. It's the oldest hockey arena in the NHL and the second oldest basketball venue in the NBA which was originally built for $1.1 billion dollars. The structure itself is a magnificent piece of architecture. It officially opened its doors to the public on February 11, 1968. The seating capacity for hockey is just over 18,000; for basketball seating capacity tips the scales at just over 19,000; and for concerts it goes even higher at 20,000 seating capacity. It offers a great behind the scenes tour of the venue, so please check its website for prices, dates, and times.

Lincoln Center for the Performing Arts -- 10 Lincoln Center Plaza -- www.lincolncenter.org

Popular among the very cultured set. It mostly offers dance, theatre, music, film, and opera performances. It is one of the most esteemed performance centers in the world. It is located in Manhattan. The New York Philharmonic, the Metropolitan Opera, and New York City Ballet also perform here. Please check their website for shows and times. It was founded by John D. Rockefeller III.

Trump Tower -- 721 Fifth Avenue

Housing the Trump Organization it is home of the soon to be 45th president of the United States Donald Trump. It's a spectacular engineering feat accented by a very nice design. It's a mix-used building which also consists of a nice atrium, offices, apartments and stores. The atrium itself has a very high ceiling and the escalator in the atrium may give you vertigo (it did to me!) due to the immensity of the lobby. This may not be accessible to visitors during the next four years as there will be a high security presence due to The Donald residing in the penthouse condominium which has many gold fixtures and designs.

PARKS AND GARDENS AND OTHER OUTDOOR SITES

There are many outdoor sites in the city of New York as well as some gorgeous parks that are worth visiting while spending time in this fabulous city. Below you will find some to put on your itinerary so you don't miss out on the grandiosity that is the world class city that is the New York metropolitan area.

Coney Island – Brooklyn, New York -- http://www.coneyisland.com/tourist-information

Open during the warmer months (approximately between the opening in Easter and the closing at Halloween), this is the most well-known amusement park in all of New York City. It's nice to visit because it has its own charm and relevance. Located on the lower peninsula, it's teeming with activity in the height of summer. A can't miss spot for couples or families. Offers 50 rides and attractions.

Central Park – located in Manhattan --
http://www.centralparknyc.org/

This is probably the most famous urban park in the entire world. So famous it was immortalized in The Rolling Stones song "Miss You" back in the seventies. This park has a zoo, walking trails, restaurants, restrooms for those who want to answer nature's call, very enticing pond, a conservatory garden, a lake, the Bethesda Fountain, a Shakespeare Garden, a visitor centre and much more. The zoo onsite has animals from temperate, tropical and polar areas of the world. Visitors are permitted to observe the daily feedings at 11:30am, 2:00pm, and 4:00pm. There is an admission fee to the zoo. You can see penguins, sea lions, goats, monkeys, and all kinds of birds of prey. This park is one of the nicest oasis you will find in any urban setting anywhere on the globe. It has been featured in such iconic shows as *Seinfeld.* The park is 750 acres in its entirety and was officially sanctioned by city officials only July 21, 1853. It receives about 37.5 million visitors every year due to its popularity.

Gramercy Park – south East 22ⁿᵈ St. just off Lexington Ave.

The park's name is both for an enclosed park and also for the neighbourhood which surrounds it. It is located in the borough of Manhattan. Only the people who reside in the neighbourhood have a key to access the park. However, the area surrounding the park is often used by joggers, people strolling with their babies, or those taking their beloved canines out for a walk. There is a Gramercy Park Hotel on site and in the park is a wonderful statue of Edwin Booth, who was a 19th century American actor who toured the country performing the works of William Shakespeare.

Bryant Park -- between 40th and 42nd Streets & Fifth and Sixth Avenues --- www.bryantpark.org

Located in Mid-town Manhattan of New York City behind the famed New York Public Library. The park is named after the late poet and editor of *The Saturday Evening Post*, William Cullen Bryant, who was also a civic reformer. He passed away in 1878 in the late 19th century. The park officially opened to the public on September 14, 1934. This is one of the most public of parks in New York as it hosts many events for the general public to enjoy. Please consult the website for what is upcoming when you will be in the city.

Battery Park – tip of Manhattan Island (no website)

This public park is located in a section of Manhattan called The Battery on the southern most tip of Manhattan Island. The name is derived from the artillery batteries that were placed there to protect the area during the early years of New York. It actually extends to New York Harbor. The area during the 17th century was primarily a Dutch Settlement when the location was known as New Amsterdam.

Brooklyn Bridge – connecting Manhattan and Brooklyn (no website)

The Brooklyn Bridge is one of the oldest in the world. It is a steel cable suspension bridge which connects the boroughs of Manhattan with Brooklyn. Completed in 1883 and opened on May 24th of that same year, it overlooks the East River. It was initially called the New York and Brooklyn Bridge followed by the East River Bridge but formally was given its present name in 1915 by those who govern the city. Its historic importance is not missed since it was recognized as a National Historic Landmark in 1964. The length of the bridge reaches almost 6,000 feet. There is no toll on the bridge and is a free thoroughfare.

Times Square – Manhattan, New York – www.timessquarenyc.org

The most famous outdoor meeting place in the world. This is the area where native New Yorkers and visitors congregate every New Year's Eve for the dropping of the proverbial crystal ball when the clock strikes midnight and then confetti galore rains down on those assembled. Near Time Square you can find hotels, restaurants, lots of shopping, Broadway, attractions and entertainment for your soul to feast on. It is highly recommended to check their website for what is in the area so you can plan your itinerary. A visit to New York is not complete without a visit to Times Square. That's like going to Italy and not seeing The Vatican. Times Square is iconic. This is the same location where the soldier famously kissed an unsuspecting female nurse after the end of World War II.

Washington Square Park – located in Greenwich Village –

www.washingtonsquareparkconservancy.org

Another very popular urban park it is located in Lower Manhattan in the very fashionable area known as Greenwich Village. Of the city's 1,900 parks it is 9.75 acres. It is a wonderful place to meet and a hub of cultural activities. Most of the buildings once home to artists now are part of New York University and have been converted into residential properties or buildings for academia. It was created in 1871. There is a notable arch as the gateway to the park and inside you will also find a very picturesque fountain.

Brooklyn Botanic Garden – it has three entrances: 150 Eastern Parkway, 455 Flatbush Avenue, 990 Washington Avenue – www.bbg.org

There is an admission price to the gardens but if you're a member admission is free of charge. The basic premise of the formation of the garden was the perseveration of horticulture and plants in the area, when the city was becoming more urbanized, and the roads were being paved over adding to the encroaching neighborhood around it. Initially it was only 39 acres but has grown since 1897 to a more elaborate 52 acres. Also offers educational programs for those interested.

New York Botanical Garden -- 2900 Southern Blvd., Bronx   -- www.nybg.org

Founded in 1891 it is 250 acre in size with over 1 million plants in its vast collection. It houses plants from temperate as well as tropical and desert locales spanning the globe. It hosts about 1 million visitors each year and offers educational programs for those with a green mind or green thumb in its conservatory. The year 2016 marks its 125 years in existence. There is a price for admission, please check its website.

Prospect Park – located in Brooklyn -- https://www.prospectpark.org

The park is quite extensive at 585 acres. It spans several neighborhoods which include Park Slope, Prospect Lefferts Gardens, Ditmas Park and Windsor Terrace, as well as Flatbush Avenue, Grand Army Plaza and the Brooklyn Botanic Garden. It is also one of the more well-known parks in the city of New York. There is a zoo on site for those who like to commune with animals. It is open year round and receives a remarkable 8 million visitors per year.

Roosevelt Island – East River, New York County (no website)

Positioned in the East River it is bordered by Manhattan on the west and Queens on the east. It is approximately 2 miles in length with a maximum width of 800 feet comprising over 147 acres. Named after former president Franklyn D. Roosevelt it earned such nicknames as Welfare Island (when it was the home of mostly hospitals), Blackwell's Island, Hog Island, and initially Minnehanonck. Most of the buildings on the island are rentals but there is also a co-op and a condominium.

DISTINCT NEIGHBORHOODS

**Little Italy – Mulberry Street --
www.littleitalynyc.com**

Initially it was where a majority of Italians live however that has transitioned to just a few Italian stores and restaurants. Its borders consist of Tribeca and Soho on the west; the Bowery and the Lower East Side on the east; Chinatown on the south; and Nolita on its northern front. The area hosts many cultural activities throughout the year such as The Feast of San Gennaro (which continues for 11 days), Carnevale, Columbus Day, and Christmas-themed events. Little Italy has been featured in many American films of the past and present.

Chinatown – Lower Manhattan, New York City
--- www.new-york-chinatown.info

The sights, the smells, the sounds, it can only be Chinatown. One of the most bustling and vibrant parks of New York there is always a myriad of activities in this part of the city. There are bargains galore to be had as well. Its borders consist of Little Italia on the north; the Civic Center on its southern tip; Tribeca to the west; and the famous Lower East Side to the east. It is the largest Chinese area in the West consisting of close to 100,000 inhabitants. New York actually has nine Chinatowns, this one is its largest. Originally populated by more Cantonese speakers the area now boasts more people who are well-versed in Mandarin. Come for the bargains and you will stay for the delicious food!

Koreatown – Midtown Manhattan (no website)

This is primarily a business district. It was spurred on by the opening of a Korean bookstore in the eighties. Those who reside in the area and are of Korean heritage number just over 200,000. The area's property values have risen due to the demand for real estate in the area. It is the second largest Korean population outside of North or South Korea. Newcomers to the area were attracted to its close proximity to sites such as Madison Square Garden, the Empire State Building, and the Garment District. The epicentre is known as Korea Way located by West 32nd Street between Fifth Avenue and Sixth Avenue where you can find some excellent stores, restaurants, karaoke bars, and spas. There are over 100 businesses located in this area.

THEATER

Broadway is the largest theater scene in the world. Also known as "The Great White Way" actors from screen and TV sometimes try their hand at some of the great shows which have been staged on Broadway or off-Broadway. One of the most recent actors to who played the Elephant Man, which was originally the purview of the late David Bowie, was the actor Bradley Cooper who gave an excellent performance. There have been more stars who have graced the stages of Broadway like Kristin Chenoweth and Idina Menzel who starred in *Wicked*. **If you would like to get some tickets at a discount for most of the shows on Broadway please check out the TKTS booth in Time Square for discounts of up to 50% on same day shows**. You can probably catch some great shows like *Book of Mormon, Matilda, Kinky Boots, Cats, Hamilton* or even *The Phantom of the Opera*.

Below is a premier comedy club and a jazz venue which might be of interest should you wish to tickle your funny bone or want to sit back and listen to some soothing jazz.

The Comedy Cellar (in Manhattan) -- 117 Macdougal Street –

www.comedycellar.com

This has to be one of the best comedy clubs in the entire world. The who's who have played in this sterling club. Some great contemporary comedians have honed their craft at the Comedy Cellar. Don't be surprised if you see some big name talent show up one night to do a gig. Aziz Ansari has showed up in the past. But, hold your hats for this! One night in January of 2017 they offered a surprise "billion dollar" show featuring Amy Shumer, Aziz Ansari, Dave Chappelle, Chris Rock, and Jerry Seinfeld. That surly was a treat for the audience!

**Blue Note Jazz Club -- 131 W 3rd Street --
www.bluenotejazz.com/newyork/index.shtml**

Probably one of the finest jazz clubs in the world.
If you're a lover of great jazz and love to sit back
and hear a renowned singer or band, this is the
place to be when you're in New York City. When
you're at the Blue Note you're amongst friends.
Please check their website for upcoming shows for
when you'll be in town. Some of the greatest in the
world of jazz have played at this fine
establishment.

SHOPPING

New York is a mecca for shopping and is a paradise when it comes to deals (especially from street vendors) or from upscale stores where you can find some of best apparel and name brand clothing around. As mentioned in "Helpful Hints" at the start of this book, please check with staff at any department stores you visit to see if there is a guest services or a tourist desk which can offer you a discount card for your purchases. Every penny saved is a penny earned, and the more you have in your pocket, the better off you will be. Since the downturn in the economy you will find that most staff is very helpful with your shopping needs.

Bloomingdales -- 59th Street and Lexington Avenue – www.bloomingdales.com

They offer translators who speak up to nine languages, have a coat and baggage check, offer personal shopping assistance and concierges, and will deliver your purchases to your hotel if they total $250 or more. One of the most revered and esteemed department stores in all of New York and the world. Up there with Harrods in England. Founded by Joseph and Lyman Bloomingdale it offers some of the most upscale shopping you will ever find. Great brand names like Perry Ellis and Ralph Lauren were initially found at stores likes Bloomingdales. Queen Elizabeth is said to be one of the patrons who have shopped at this department store.

Saks Fifth Avenue -- 611 -- 5TH AVENUE – www.saksfifthavenue.com

Now owned by one of the oldest and largest retailing giants, the Canadian company named the Hudson's Bay Company, it has outposts in Toronto and Ottawa in Canada. It's located on Fifth Avenue in Mid-town Manhattan. It offers jewelry, shoes, apparel, hand bags, and accessories mostly with designer names. The product line is for both males and females. Saks was founded in the early 1900s by Horace Saks and Bernard Gimbel. You would be able to find such revered names as Gucci and Valentino here.

Macy's Herald Square -- 151 W 34th St. -- http://l.macys.com/new-york-ny

Famous for putting on the Macy's Thanksgiving Day Parade which has been a landmark in the lore of New York City, this legendary department store is a must-see and a must-visit for anyone who's visiting. Offers clothes for women, men and kids. Its product line extends to beauty, apparel, accessories, shoes, handbags, watches, bed and bath items, and furniture and mattresses. The staff is very helpful and some are very friendly and will engage you in a light conversation if given the opportunity.

J.C. Penney -- 92-59 59th Ave, Queens Centre (1st location) and 100 W 32nd St., Manhattan Mall (2nd location) -- www.jcpenney.com

Another one of the famous department stores which is significant to the New York City retailing establishments. It has been a favorite amongst New Yorkers and to those visiting the city. One location is close to Koreatown, that's the one located in

Manhattan. Offers clothing for all members of the family for both men and women, adolescents, and kids. Its product line goes from jewelry to handbags, appliances to shoes, and also other accoutrements for the home like for the bath and bedroom. Stores are open seven days a week for those eager to get some shopping done. Can ship to Canada as well as across the United States.

SOME SELECTED RESTAURANTS

The scope and immensity of all the restaurants in New York are so vast it would be hard to include them in just one book. Of course, you also have some that close and new ones which open. You can almost find any kind of culinary delight from anywhere across the globe somewhere in New York City. The city's restaurant scene is one of the most eclectic compared to most cities in the world. That's what makes dining in New York such a gastronomic adventure. Here are just some suggestions which might be able to give you a very small impression of what it has to offer. (Please note: there was an excellent Italian restaurant called Rocco's which was located in Greenwich Village which was supposed to be on my list but has since closed. It was a gem and will, sadly, be missed.)

FOR BREAKFAST

If you don't want to pay the steep price of having breakfast at your hotel there is always a good **Starbucks** to be found. Many offer some excellent bagels and other options for the first meal of the day. They, of course, offer some excellent juices, great coffee, and teas. And, yes, if you want two tea bags in your tea just request it. There is a Starbucks almost everywhere you turn in New York. They also offer paninis and sandwiches. For those who like their dairy there are also yogurt and fruit. There are cold drinks which are offered as well. Ice coffee, anyone?! **www.starbucks.com**

FOR BREAKFAST, LUNCH OR DINNER

Raffles Bistro -- 511 Lexington Avenue at 48th Street (in Manhattan)

Attached to The Lexington in Manhattan it is one of the most vivacious restaurants I've been to. The restaurant during peak times like breakfast, lunch, or dinner is buzzing with activity. The food is absolutely amazing and the staff is very friendly. It is a bit on the pricey side but it is well worth it. The portions are fairly large your appetite will be satiated in no time. It's not the largest restaurant but the experience of dining there is an experience you will not regret!

FOR LUNCH OR DINNER

Quality Meats -- 57 W 58th St. (in Manhattan) -- http://www.qualitymeatsnyc.com/home.cfm

If you love steak and good wine this is the restaurant for you. Located in the heart of Manhattan it is always very busy due to its popularity. If you have gluten allergies they can also accommodate you as well. Also offers chicken and seafood for those who are not into beef. Great appetizers and desserts as well. I would highly recommend making a reservation if you plan to dine at this fine establishment.

Sardi's -- 234 W 44th St # 3 -- www.sardis.com

One of the most famous of New York City landmarks, it is very well-known for having caricatures of American celebrity luminaries gracing its walls. It's almost as popular as the Empire State Building. Open for lunch or dinner and has prix fix menus as well for pre- or post-theater guests. The restaurant has made some appearances in some Hollywood films as well. Great wine list and desserts are also found on the menu.

Tavern on the Green -- Central Park West & 67th Street -- www.tavernonthegreen.com

Has been serving patrons since 1934 and is another of New York's most iconic restaurants. During the spring, summer, and fall if there is good weather you can dine al fresco on the patio, or during the other times of year there is excellent dining indoors. Offers chicken, seafood, burgers and steaks. Soup and salads are also on the menu. A great place to dine if you want to say "I've been there!" Excellent ambience too!

Katz's Delicatessen -- 205 East Houston Street (corner of Ludlow St) -- www.katzsdelicatessen.com

This is one of the most important restaurants in all of New York. With the closing of the Carnegie Deli at the end of 2016, this remains the premiere resto to get some of the most amazing deli sandwiches in all of New York City. Originally opened in 1888 under a different name this current iteration of the restaurant was officially founded in 1917. It is located on the Lower East Side. Has some great pastrami, salami, and other deli sandwiches for you to enjoy and savour! Northeast of Little Italy and east of Lower Manhattan.

Olive Garden – www.olivegarden.com

There are several across New York City. If you would like some good Italian food but not the steep prices this might be your best bet. I have young American relatives who swear by it. It's their go-to for something that is not too expensive but still very appetizing.

FAST FOOD

Yes, there are numerous **McDonald's**, **Burger Kings**, and **Wendy's** in New York. But if you would like something more on the exotic side try **Chipotle**. They did have some problems in the past but which has since been alleviated. Chipotle's salads and burritos are amazing! They really know how to make them. It's great if you're just looking for a good inexpensive lunch or if you would like a snack late in the evening after dinner. You could also opt for street meats like the ubiquitous hot dog from a vendor if you just want something to tide you over between lunch and dinner.

SOURCES

This guide book was carefully assembled from the author's seven trips to New York City over four decades; articles in three newspapers (*Toronto Star, The New York Times,* and *Metro*); interviews and recommendations from friends and relatives (some who are native New Yorkers); and some web searches to verify some information.

About the author: Michael Persaud is a freelance writer who formerly worked for over two decades in the tourism industry. He currently writes for *The Downsview Advocate*. He has published over 20 ebooks and books. He has also written for numerous newspapers over the years including the largest newspaper in Canada by circulation, the *Toronto Star*. He is also past president of T.O.P.S. (The Ontario Poetry Society). If you like this book you might like some of his other titles which include *Toronto: A Complete Guide on the City*; *The Beatles*; *A Canadian Childhood*; *How To Save More Money*; *How To Win*

Friends Easily; or *The Love and Power of Reading*. He would like to express his gratitude to you for purchasing this book!

Printed in Great Britain
by Amazon

35267934R00052